wowisms

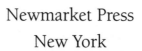

Newmarket Press

New York

wowisms

Words of Wisdom for Dreamers and Doers

RON RUBIN
and
STUART AVERY GOLD

MINISTERS OF
The REPUBLIC of TEA

FIRST EDITION
ISBN 1-55704-590-9
1 2 3 4 5 6 7 8 9 10

Library of Congress Cataloging-in-Publication Data

Wowisms : words of wisdom for dreamers and doers / [compiled by] Ron
Rubin and Stuart Avery Gold. —1st ed.
    p. cm.
 ISBN 1-55704-590-9 (alk. paper)
1. Success—Psychological aspects. 2. Change (Psychology) 3. Risk-taking
(Psychology) I. Rubin, Ron. II. Gold, Stuart Avery.
BF637.S8W7 2003
  158—dc22

                              2003018731

QUANTITY PURCHASES
Companies, professional groups, clubs, and other organizations
may qualify for special terms when ordering quantities of this title.
For information, write Special Sales, Newmarket Press,
18 East 48th Street, New York, NY 10017,
call (212) 832-3575 or (800) 669-3903, or fax (212) 832-3629.
www.newmarketpress.com

Manufactured in the United States of America.
At the authors' request, this book has been
printed on acid-free paper.

A NOTE FROM THE PUBLISHER

When the opportunity arose to publish Ron and Stuart's first Zentrepreneur Guide, *Success at Life*, I believed that their unique approach to life and business would resonate with creative, entrepreneurial spirits everywhere. And I was right. Letters from excited readers poured in—Ron and Stuart had moved people to pursue their passions, to "live a dream defined," to become Zentrepreneurs.

Dragon Spirit followed *Success at Life* two years later, and even more affirming letters and e-mails poured in, as well as offers from publishers in Russia, Portugal, Israel, and Greece to translate the books in their languages. Sayings and phrases from the books were being exchanged by fans and jotted on bulletin boards and diaries.

As I was the first editor to read the manuscript over four years ago, you might understandably ask me, "When you first read the pages Stuart sent you, how did you know this could become a book that would connect to others the way it has?" Well, one answer is that it's my job, and the job of all book editors, to draw on their experience and intuition to evaluate submissions, work with writers, and recommend for publication what they believe will resound with readers.

The other, more personal answer is that the manuscript spoke to me. I discovered that I too was a Zentrepreneur. You see, 21 years ago, I left the corporate publishing world to found my own independent company. I started Newmarket in my apartment, publishing two books the first year, five the next, and now, with a wonderful, dedicated staff, we publish about 30 books a year and have over 250 titles in print. I encountered many dreamkillers along the way, and still do. So, what's wonderful about *Success at Life* and *Dragon Spirit* for me, and perhaps for you, is that they put into words what I need to read or hear to help me meet the challenges that come with being a Zentrepreneur, especially on those days when everything feels like a battle and faith is hard to come by.

I've highlighted many phrases in the books, as have many other readers. Which is what led to Book #3 in the Zentrepreneur Guide series: *Wowisms*, a treasury of what the authors call "proverbs of possibility that will ennoble your spirit, initiate your mind, and encourage an awakening that engages and guides you to embrace your fullest essence and unlimited potential."

I founded Newmarket on the principle that we would identify and publish books and authors with unique merit, and I'm very proud to add this new book, *Wowisms*, to our growing list. Enjoy—and dare to dream!

Esther Margolis, Founder, President & Publisher
Newmarket Press, August 2003

For Andy

"Believe nothing, no matter where you read it, or who said it, no matter if I have said it, unless it agrees with your own reason and your own common sense." —Buddha

INTERVAL

At first there is no road. It's only when a person begins it that it exists for others.

WHAT FOLLOWS is very much true. Beginning with I've never read anything I've written. Not after it's been published. Not once. Not ever.

Not so with Ron.

He's been known to visit with our pages from time to time, preparing for an appearance, lecture, or interview.

He has even read passages aloud when invited to do so. Never minding, glad to oblige, gracious—always that, so much so a gent, that's Ron. But that's not me. Can't do it.

Oh, I read and reread what I've put down during the keyboard-clacking process of writing a book. Ceaselessly shaping and shading. Striving for the right word in the right place. Wondering what works, what doesn't, trying very hard to make the concepts Ron and I have developed interesting and inspiring—thought-connecting, too. Always hoping that it is written well, praying that it is accepted well. Blissfully happy that after so many months that something exists. Mostly terrified that once it's polished and put out there for public view, that each day that dawns, zero people on planet Earth will care. Just another vestigial waste of pulp, lost on the bookseller's shelf, gasping for air, of interest to no one. (Pssst! While you snore with happiness, this is the nightmare of all writers, the sort of madness that haunts our dreams the most.)

Closing in, this is not a confidence thing. Hardly. Hold me upside down and give me a good shake and believe me, confidence will pour out of my ears. But still, I pretty much never begin a page without cursing my lack of talent, or end one successfully dodging my helplessness. Because regardless of what happens later, no matter how much sales are going good, the books booming, pleasing the publisher and giddying those that own their stock, no matter how kind and assuring the plaudits and reviews, I long ago realized something, which in the interest of accuracy, I will share with you now. Shhh. . .

I could have done better.

This is the torment I keep inside. My inner reality. That the ideas and intellections that were so golden in my mind back when, the thoughts that were winged with such purpose and passion, when they circle and land, becoming ink on paper, in part of my head I know that I could have done, well, just so much better. That's where my mind goes spinning away to hide when I think about my writing.

Denigrating further, I have no problem sharing with you yet another of my nutball lunacies, which is the fear that many, most, who might turn to our books for guidance, inspiration, or enlightenment would discover the experience to be nothing more than an aberration, and that's the panic I live with regardless of their praise unending.

So again, since I don't much care for my writing, I've never read anything I've written. Not after it's been published. Not once. Not ever. Because even though no one will ever know how hard I slaved, always, always turning in only my best work, wanting whatever I write to have as much quality as possible, I know in my heart of hearts that I could have done better. And how do I deal with such beveiled expectation? Easy.

As a Zentrepreneur, I not only know that I can always do better—I believe it. And understand this: Believing is a Zentrepreneur's most prized possession.

While some live the life they've been given, Zentrepreneurs live the life they believe in.

For that is what Zentrepreneurs are: believers who believe in living a life in which what they do is one with what they are. Pursuing their passion for the possible, perceiving a clarity of purpose, Zentrepreneurs endeavor to study and practice, to live a life where the creative spark, the inner illumination of spirit, talent, and uniqueness, is put into motion, fostering growth that not only enriches their own life, but the lives of others as well. But more than that, Zentrepreneurs have made their lives noble and rich beyond counting by living a dream defined. Exuberantly so. And how do they get to a place of such happiness and light, where they have the courage and commitment to follow their feelings and live a life where they can take charge, create, and do? By simply doing no less than one thing only—

Believing they can.

Which is what we all need to do. All of us. All of the time.

This book was born of a belief that every time someone finds his or her own way, he or she paves the way for someone else. That to journey our best life we need only to begin on a path of enlightenment, but realize, please, that the path to achieving your deserved greatness cannot be taught, it must be taken. Only then can illumination be delivered.

Enter Federal Express.

There is a profound Japanese proverb that states: "To teach is to learn." I learned a tremendously meaningful lesson one fortuitous midmorning, beginning innocently enough, with a package that came to me that day. At first, the contents were common enough. A book. One of ours. A very well-worn Zentrepreneur's Guide with just the most beautiful note along with.

Here it is, verbatim.

Dear Ron and Stuart,

Blessings to you for writing this book. I could never express how wonderful, good and true your teachings, inspiration and advice have been and continue to be for me. Your words have given me the life-enhancing encouragement to take the steps I have been wanting to take for years. It could have never come along at a better time in my life and I refer to the pages on a daily basis. (Note the extensive use of yellow high-lighter. The book's condition due to my reading it over and over while working out on a treadmill.) It would mean just so much if you could both take the time to sign this for me. I wish there were more people like you in this world to teach us to live our passion and our dreams and not to look back. Your empowering words of wisdom have changed me and I will carry them with me throughout my journeys in life.

Well, now. I don't know what you might think after reading such a letter, so thoughtful and sin-cere, and thank you very much, but I can tell you how it triggered Ron and me.

Blew us away.

And want to know what? This marvelous incident permanently altered my view, forcing me, for the first time, surprisingly and stunningly to read a few of the jottings I've put down, not only with fresh eyes, but more importantly, through the eyes of another.

And want to know what else? The way this person had descended on the pages of the book, embracing them, isolating so many passages with such obvious focus and satisfying belief, the luminous flash of yellow highlighter holding them bright to the light, the way it was done, I realized she had to be serious when she said the encounter with our words had changed her.

Changed me, too.

Enough to look back a bit at some of the stuff I've written, the climactic moment, alas, not too terrible, the excursion allowing me to recognize something that, trapped in my own skin, I could not see before—the unimportance of trying to build a church out of my words. I was confusing content with contentment, missing the true whisper of the words that within the stillness spoke a message as old as the world: By doing something that may help to change the circumstances of others, we help to change the circumstances of ourselves.

This book is about change. More to the point, it is a book about the ultimate dynamic of life, your innate capacity to change your circumstance, perspective, and direction, indeed the power that is yours to become the change you wish to be. It is our fervent hope that this gathering of Wowisms—these proverbs of possibility—will ennoble your spirit, initiate your mind, and encourage an awakening that engages and guides you to embrace your fullest essence and unlimited potential. Change is the elixir of life. Open yourself to the wow and the wonder— the renewal it can bring—remembering always, please, that you get the life that you allow. And so, as we get started, let me say, may you all become dreamers and doers and may you also remember this: While some books change the way you think, some books change the way you live. Either way. . .

Over to you.

—*Stuart Avery Gold*

No dream is impossible if you just dare to live it.

DISCOVERING your passion will ignite the fire and fan the flames of your dreams and desires. Living your passion will put the world on notice that you are different. Different because your life is more purposeful, fulfilling, joyous, and exciting. Passion provides you with the best possible odds to successfully catch and live your dream.

By having the courage to risk rejection and failure, you provide yourself with the wondrous opportunity to succeed.

You are here for a reason.
You were born with an innate
capability to do, be, and have all
that your heart yearns for.

You must be the relentless architect of your own unique possibilities.

THE meaning is in the dreaming.

Your future is not determined by luck, it's determined by the actions you take each and every day. Successful people do the things that unsuccessful people are not willing to do.

ONLY those who risk something achieve something.

How old would you be if you didn't know how old you were? No matter. It's never too late to have the life you want to live.

SUCCESS only comes to people who grasp it, and wisdom is the all-important thing that extends your reach.

LET the dream be present and you will become genuine. Let it guide you and you will flourish. Let it become a reality and you will become one with the Universe.

IT is your personal responsibility to reaffirm your commitment to your commitment.

WITH a passionate determination to succeed you will not be defeated.

THE natural way is the way.
Those who know the journey path
know the way to yield. To yield is to
become. Only then will the true way
of the Universe be observed. For it
is the way.

To move on, sometimes the best light for the journey can be the result of a burning bridge.

ZENTREPRENEURS embrace the process of life, allowing themselves to be taken with the spiritual energies of the Universe, knowing that they too are part of the unity of all things.

KNOW that within us all, we possess a unique essence—a self-enhancing actualizing power—to master our own destiny.

A healthy mind and body is the true incontestable currency of success.

W<small>ED</small> being and doing.

To live your dream, you must embark on a pilgrimage of clarity and personal growth, welcoming the practices, techniques, and principles that will awaken the sensory awareness that lies within and without you.

KNOW beyond all question that you
are a universal presence, a miraculous
being endowed with gifts and with
purpose that will allow you to become
who you envision yourself to be.

PASSION breeds excitement, excitement breeds success.

ONLY by embracing your passions can you achieve the satisfaction and joy in life you are destined for.

Do you believe what you see, or do you see what you believe?

A dream is not an *it*, it is an *us*, our spiritual signature, a life force that is greater than ourselves, that works itself through us, awakening the soul, rhythming the heart, and allowing for the changing and growing self.

W<small>HILE</small> entrepreneurs get hold of an idea, Zentrepreneurs let an idea get hold of them.

IT isn't the mind that possesses an idea—it is the idea that possesses the mind.

CHANGE, like the beauty of a flower,
is ordinary activity.

GOOD advice is always there for us, if we are simply there for it.

ONLY those who know they know not
can become wise.

WORK and life are an interconnected adventure, guided by the heart, winged with spirit, and nourished by the soul.

ZENTREPRENEURS endeavor to live a
life in which what they do is one with
what they are.

THE actions you take today will determine your tomorrows. In order for success to occur, you must create a sense of urgency to do—to act on the great idea for your life. To delay in taking direct, assertive action is to relinquish your well-deserved right to achieve your deepest desires. No matter what time of day you check your watch, the only time is now.

To live a life of gladness, all any of us have to do is make a conscious decision about the future and the glorious wonders we want to create, realizing that while tragically so many people make the mistake of waiting for happiness, happiness is always here, waiting for us.

THE Universe is for us and with us. Embrace it, without holding on. It is our invitation to partake of infinity.

CHANGE is the elixir of life.

CHANGE is nothing more than the gathering of energy that the Universe constantly recycles, allowing for the limitless possibilities that it holds for us.

BECOME better human beings by being like bamboo, dealing with events directly and adapting with the endurance to change as need be. While the strongest tree can be uprooted and knocked over in a storm, bamboo prevails in adverse conditions, by bending and yielding to the prevailing winds.

GRACEFUL and assured under pressure, bamboo moves easily with the shifts of circumstance, all the while retaining its own innate and effortless strength.

Mᴇᴇᴛ sudden changes in life with a disposition of vitality and flexibility. Flexibility masters difficulty. Meet change! Greet change! Merge with it! Mold it! Evolve with it! Morph with it! Become harmoniously one with it. Be the change you wish to see. Become the person you were meant to be.

TAKE what you have and have what it takes to make your life an exhilarating opus of radiance for yourself and all those who you come in contact with.

Risk is the glue that binds us to the possibility of success.

IT is not what you may *get* from taking a risk, but rather what you *become* because of taking it.

IF you make each effort a masterpiece,
know that the gods can do no better.

By piloting your passion, by specializing in self-optimization, the energy you give will equal the energy you get, allowing you to achieve a more fulfilling and gracious existence.

PAINT your passion, so others may believe. Live your passion, so that you may succeed.

MORE than any specific skill or talent, turning a dream into a reality requires placing priority on certain qualities of thought and attitude.

SUCCESS is not the attribute of a blessed special few—it is the endowment of all who open themselves to inspiration, desire, and hard work.

Do not expend time imagining *what might* happen as a result of your effort, but rather imagine what it is that you can *actually make happen* as a result of your effort.

WHATEVER your talent, idea, product, business, or service, whatever it is that you have or bring, you must commit to setting your compass to amaze anew by showing all that you are somehow in some way *different*.

To journey the path of success, it doesn't matter where you are or where you have been. The marvel of the pilgrimage is that it has only to do with where you are going. And to get there, you need only start right where you are.

$A_{PTITUDE}$ + Attitude = Altitude

STOP waiting for permission.
You were born with the permission
to be yourself.

BEFORE you can move others, you must first move yourself.

KNOW that the surest way not to fail is to believe that you will succeed!

SEEK more than others think is wise.

Risk more than others think is safe.

Know that the only limitations in life

are the ones you place on yourself.

WITH desire, dedication, and perseverance, the vision you see will become what can be.

CONCEIVE. Believe. Achieve.

SUCCESS comes to those who grasp it.

ANY success you achieve will come
only as a result of any action you
undertake.

DON'T just go with life, grow with life.

Your success is not determined by luck, it's determined by the actions you choose to take each and every day.

A dream is a powerful nexus that attaches the mind to the soul, allowing you to create your personal purpose, your vision of what is truly important to you. By empowering your creative imagination, you cross over the shadow threshold to future possibilities.

P<small>ASSION</small> in. Passion out.

WHILE the entrepreneur pretends
to know what's next, a Zentrepreneur
imagines what's next. And believes
in it deeply.

NEVER let go the wonder.

K<small>NOWLEDGE</small> is the oxygen of success.

KNOWLEDGE is the animating breath that brings the cosmos closer and allows you to grasp the possibilities and promise that awaits.

EACH piece of knowledge leads to the next.

WISDOM is a weight that is carried easily.

KNOWLEDGE enables you to forge ahead and do battle with the unknown.

IF you know that you do not know everything, then you know everything you need to know.

THE next best thing to having knowledge is knowing where and how to find it.

WHILE Western medicine insists that it is the brain that moves the body, the Zentrepreneur knows that it is the mind that moves the world. The ongoing trouble is that since always humans have tried to squeeze the mind into the brain, never realizing that it won't fit.

Uncover wisdom. Develop direction.
Become a connoisseur of capability.
A catalyst for change. Enable yourself
to take the dares. Success is an act of
exploration. A commitment to a quest
to be the best.

WISDOM, not capital, is the quintessential currency needed to champion your idea.

ONLY by looking into your self, recognizing your potential, and tapping into your qualities of passion and purpose can you actualize all that you will need to set the great idea of your life free, forever directing your destiny.

WHEN it comes to living your dream,
whether you think you will or won't—
you're right.

How your life unfolds depends on the choices you make. Choosing to go with your natural expression, following your true calling, will allow you to discover clarity and commitment, the things that give ideas shape and substance and provide you with the gift of harmonious living.

WHEN you seek your dream,
you seek yourself.

F~AILURE~ is the lubricant of success.

ONCE you have determined your life's mission, let no failure keep you from your goal.

Dare to do. Only by opening
your heart and your mind will you
experience the joy and contentment
of being fully alive.

NEVER ever surrender the great idea for your life.

WITHIN you lies the power that can make the invisible visible and the intangible the real. Use your mind, do not let your mind use you. Summon your instinct.

Your dream may be dismissed, derided, disparaged, and cruelly ridiculed, but it cannot be taken away unless it is given up on.

THERE are certain absolute truths on this planet and one of them is that the mind can play tricks, but the heart cannot be fooled.

BELIEVE in the great idea for your life,
knowing that there is an idea for every
time and a time for every idea.

WHILE some make the mistake of wasting time and money on the process of positioning an idea, others understand that success comes from the process of positioning themselves.

IDEAS are opportunities.
Serendipitous openings for glory and
joy, waiting for that certain individual
whose unique time it is to deliver them
out of the darkness.

You must commit yourself fully to manifesting your ability. But understand that wanting to will not be enough. Willing to will not be enough. There is no will or want, there is only to do. You must do in order to master the circumstances of life or risk having the circumstances of life master you.

M_{ASTERING} your inner world allows
you to master the outer world.

DISCIPLINE is the seed of success that will germinate the deep roots to inner-power, the virtue incarnate that permits you to block out those voices that create tremendous tension, insecurity, fear, and doubt and allow a unity of purpose and mind, a focus on listening to the authentic, meaningful dialogue of your own heart.

Do not let others block your light.

ADHERE to the ecstatic rhythms and metrics of what you aspire to.

LEARN to listen to what wants to happen—get completely involved with the inner voice that seeks to be heard. The opportunity that it presents is a path to self-realization. The symbiosis of possibility and purpose awaits to marshal creation. Creation is everything—life is everything. There is no separating the two. Therefore, creation is life and life is creation.

Empower yourself to power yourself.
Accept personal responsibility for
expending the energy to take on the
essential tasks needed to fulfill
your dream.

A Zentrepreneur's mind is limitless, its potential inexhaustible. And once you understand that the brain cannot hold the mind, you free yourself to turn your dream into a radiant reality.

Too many are focused on their fiscal fitness, ignoring the absolute importance of their physical fitness.

YOUR well-being is your greatest asset.

Do not choose between mind and body, but choose both mind and body.

To live your dream, you don't need to change yourself, you need only to change your life.

YOUR dream can and will come true if you focus on your desire to go from where you are to where you want to be.

ACCEPT the ups and downs as natural events and use them as welcomed lessons that facilitate self-transcendence and growth.

STRIVE for excellence and not perfection.

ATTENTION is guided by intention
and held steady by will.

Your power to control your thoughts is the power to re-create your circumstance.

THERE is nothing that cannot be gotten rid of, no burden that cannot be lifted, no care that cannot be dissolved, by taking the time to experience the life that is in front of us. Awaken yourself. Be grateful. Take notice of the marvel, the perfection, the natural serenity, and the true esthetic in every moment and every thing that daily life offers.

EMBRACE the wonder and the wonderment of daily life.

Do not take for granted how superb
even the smallest pleasure life extends.

WHILE there are limits to the time we all have to live our lives, there are no limits on how we live our time.

BE mindful of the moment.

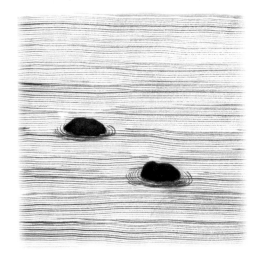

PRACTICE a life of passion, where what you want to do is one with what you do.

HAVE more than a spherical awareness
of your world, understanding the
sweet joy that all future is perpetually
in motion and that you have within
you the power of inspired purpose—
the force to create, manifest, and
deliver whatever it is you want to
accomplish in this world.

BELIEVE fully in the divine magic of your talents and gifts—trust that there is an allotted place in this world for what you want to accomplish. Your ideas and dreams are a necessary thread in the weave of fabric that is the material of the Universe.

NOTHING external, no adversity, difficulty, or doubt, can have any power over you unless you allow it to. You are deserving and have the power within to live with passion and intention.

Have confidence in the bounty
of your imagination and follow your
instincts.

LIVE in the openness of possibility.

CHOOSING to move yourself with full heart and mind has the ability to move others—indeed it is what spins the galaxies.

SURRENDER yourself to awareness.

WHILE some follow a rainbow,
others create one.

THE path to success reveals itself to those who have the wisdom to see it.

THERE is nothing elusive about your ability to turn your most desired dream into a living reality; it is your birthright, an endowment given you once you stop searching outside for answers that lie within.

LIVING the life you imagine is not something to be acquired by outer means, rather it is a total awakening to the capacity of your own true nature that is the start of everything.

Too much of life is spent on looking for the right answers, when the secret to life lies in being able to ask the right questions. It is the questions we ask or fail to ask that shape our path.

THE way is not a thing to be conquered; rather it is an ongoing process that ennobles fully what you are capable of.

You can realize the greatness of
your dream by simply possessing the
unwavering confidence to realize
the greatness of your self.

IN order to create a fulfilling future, you must first envision or dream it. Dreams are your creative vision, a way to explore, expand, and redefine the infinite possibilities of your life.

WHEN the world becomes too little or too much, endure with persistence. Know that the way to endure is to have the strength to yield, to change course as need be.

Too often people look desperately outside their lives for what they want when the creative power to build their best life lies within.

To live a dream delighted is not some rare privilege handed only to others who are more gifted, luckier, or more advantaged than you. It is the primal birthright belonging to every man and woman who does not resist discovery of the ocean of bliss, realizing that to enter the stream of happiness, you have simply to flow with it.

SAY yes to the courage and confidence to live the life that you were meant to live. Dare to dream. Dream to dare. Be bold. Let your imagination proffer possibilities and ignite your passions. Allow WOW.

EMBRACE your imaginative power and do not resist letting in that which wants to be let in.

HAPPINESS is screaming for us, if only we would quiet ourselves long enough to listen.

LEARN to think different and you will discover the different.

ZENTREPRENEURS have unconditional
self-regard. Trusting his or her own
instincts, they spend little or no time
thinking about what they can't do and
instead think entirely in terms of what
they *can* and *must* do to catch and
live their dreams.

BEGIN to believe you can move a mountain. Believe you can move others. Know you can move yourself.

You are at all times sublime, each moment standing at the crossroads of what is and what can be.

BECOME a provocateur of potential.
Dream big. Size matters. Dream wild.
Boundlessness matters.

Do not let the unexpected act on you.
Act on the unexpected.

A Zentrepreneur realizes that the secret to the magic life is to recognize that the way the Universe works is the way we work, for the Universe is us, always becoming itself, at the same time like us, changing into something else.

Aᴄᴛ as if you will.

THE will and the willingness come from within. Success manifests from the inside out.

SUCCESS is not man-made.

It's mind-made.

ACCEPT yourself for not knowing
and you simplify the journey.

ALL is possible if you will only make
a courageous commitment to rely
upon yourself. No one else can journey
the path for you. It is you who must
walk in expectancy, counting only on
yourself to be the relentless architect
of your destiny.

OTHERS may change the way you live,
but only you can change your life.

DREAM 10,000 dreams knowing that 10,000 dreams is only the beginning.

To be totally rich, strive for the
things that money can't buy.

THE truer journey is to become
someone, not something.

WHEN you can no longer distinguish
the dream from the reality you have
learned how to live.

AT first there is no road. It's only when a person begins it that it exists for others.

Be unreasonable. Hang on to a tenacity that others may regard as an upside-down belief, until the world looks level. Persistence gives timing a chance to come to your aid.

P~ATIENCE~ is continued effort.

INTUITION is the delicious fruit of solitude.

RESISTANCE, distraction, and fear:
These are merely things that become
visible when you take your eyes off
your dream.

YOUR inner reservoir of commitment
is the difference between a strong will
and a strong won't.

CREATING a stalwart, undaunted attitude is the single most important ingredient in your recipe for success.

Live to dream. Dream to live. Let the sphere of yin and yang combine. By polishing consciousness true destiny emerges. Having refined the luminous spirit, discover the ancient secret of happiness.

YOUR mind, like the future, is only what you make of it.

ABOUT THE AUTHORS

RON RUBIN AND STUART AVERY GOLD are "Ministers" of *The Republic of Tea*, one of the most successful and fastest growing cachet brands in America today. Headquartered in Novato, California, *The Republic of Tea* sells the finest teas and herbs in the world to specialty food and select department stores, cafés, and restaurants and through its award-winning mail order catalog and Website: www.republicoftea.com

RON RUBIN, the "Minister of Tea," is Chairman of the Board of *The Republic of Tea*. He keeps a permanent residence in Clayton, Missouri.

STUART AVERY GOLD, the "Minister of Travel," is COO and the lauded editorial "voice" for the company's Tea Revolution. He keeps a permanent residence in Boca Raton, Florida.

ACKNOWLEDGMENTS

This book would not be if it weren't for the many and more dreamers turned doers who have written us from around the world. We thank each and all.

To Gina Amador our designer superb, for always envisioning and creating.

A special thank you to Machiko for the beautiful MindScapes.

To Aaryn for her sumi-e ink interpretation.

To everyone at Newmarket Press for helping us stay on the path, especially Keith Hollaman, Shannon Berning, Heidi Sachner, Harry Burton, MaryJane DiMassi, Tom Perry, Paul Sugarman, Frank DeMaio, and to William Rusin and Dosier Hammond of W.W. Norton & Company.

To our treasure of a publisher, Esther Margolis, for her heart and instinct, confidence and push. She has been, and always is, everything grand.

SHARE THE JOURNEY

Tell us your story

As the proud publisher of this book, we hope that you have been inspired to discover the Zentrepreneur in you. The fact that you purchased this book proves that you are open to your limitless potential. If someone gave you this book, it proves that someone recognizes your limitless potential. We invite you to share with us your thoughts and experiences about becoming a Zentrepreneur. The best contributors and their stories may even be used in future Zentrepreneur Guides®.

Keep up-to-date

If you'd like to stay abreast of Zentrepreneur Guide® publications and activities, join our mailing list (we don't sell or pass on mailing list information). See below for where to send your name and email or address.

All Zentrepreneur Guide® correspondence should be sent to:

> Zentrepreneur Guides®
> Newmarket Press
> 18 E. 48th Street
> New York, NY 10017

Ron and Stuart can be reached at www.zentrepreneurs.com

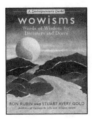
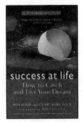